MANAGING P

MW01680351

This No Nonsense Guide Will Show You:

- ★ How to become a management P•R•O
- ★ The best ways to deal with your boss, subordinates, business associates, family, and friends
- ★ The way to become more organized
- ★ How to get ahead—in business, with family, in life

THE NO NONSENSE LIBRARY

NO NONSENSE CAREER GUIDES

How to Use Your Time Wisely
Managing People

NO NONSENSE FINANCIAL GUIDES

How to Finance Your Child's College Education
How to Use Credit and Credit Cards, Revised Edition
Understanding Tax-Exempt Bonds, Revised Edition
Understanding Money Market Funds, Revised Edition
Understanding Mutual Funds, Revised Edition
Understanding IRA's, Revised Edition
Understanding Treasury Bills and Other U.S. Government Securities, Revised Edition
Understanding Common Stocks, Revised Edition
Understanding the Stock Market, Revised Edition
Understanding Stock Options and Futures Markets, Revised Edition
How to Choose a Discount Stockbroker, Revised Edition
How to Make Personal Financial Planning Work for You, Revised Edition
How to Plan and Invest for Your Retirement, Revised Edition
The New Tax Law and What It Means to You

NO NONSENSE REAL ESTATE GUIDES

Understanding Condominiums and Co-ops, Revised Edition
Understanding Buying and Selling a House, Revised Edition
Understanding Mortgages and Home Equity Loans, Revised Edition
Refinancing Your Mortgage, Revised Edition

NO NONSENSE LEGAL GUIDES

Understanding Estate Planning and Wills, Revised Edition
How to Choose a Lawyer

NO NONSENSE SUCCESS GUIDES

NO NONSENSE HEALTH GUIDES

NO NONSENSE COOKING GUIDES

NO NONSENSE PARENTING GUIDES

NO NONSENSE WINE GUIDES

NO NONSENSE CAREER GUIDE™

MANAGING PEOPLE AT WORK♦ AT HOME

Phyllis C. Kaufman
& Arnold Corrigan

Longmeadow Press

Managing People At Work ♦ At Home

Cover art by Bets, Ltd.
Production services by William S. Konecky Associates, New York.

Published by Longmeadow Press, 201 High Ridge Road, Stamford, Connecticut 06904.

ISBN: 0-681-40140-0

Printed in the United States of America

0 9 8 7 6 5 4 3 2 1

TO

ABBE AND PERRY LEFF, WITH LOVE

CONTENTS

ACKNOWLEDGMENTS

The authors want to thank William J. Doyle, Chairman of the Board, Hill International, Inc. and Herbert M. Adler, M.D., Clinical Professor, Departments of Family Medicine and Psychiatry, Thomas Jefferson University, for sharing their knowledge, expertise, and insight in the preparation of this book.

INTRODUCTION

The No Nonsense Career Guide, *Managing People at Work ♦ at Home* is about understanding, communicating, and dealing with people. The scope of this book is broad—dealing with those you work with and those you love—because, with few exceptions, the techniques for dealing successfully with all people are surprisingly similar.

You will learn the No Nonsense P*R*O PLUS Management system. P*R*O stands for Priority/Reward Organizer. A P*R*O is someone who can analyze priorities according to potential rewards and organize them so that the most time is devoted to items with the highest reward potential.

But being a P*R*O is not the complete answer to being a successful people manager. That skill comes when you practice P*R*O PLUS, the combination of priority/reward organization PLUS respecting the self-esteem of those with whom you deal.

In Part I, we introduce you to the P*R*O system, giving you a method or plan to follow yourself and in your interpersonal dealings. In Part II, we'll take P*R*O and add to it the PLUS principle of respecting self-esteem. In subsequent parts, we'll apply P*R*O PLUS to various situations at work and at home. And finally, in Part V, we'll discuss time management, the art of making the most out of the opportunities P*R*O PLUS presents.

PART I

P*R*O

1 · BE A MANAGEMENT P*R*O

A good manager is a good self-manager. No one can be an effective manager of others until he/she understands how to manage him/herself. We begin Part I by applying P•R•O to you.

P•R•O stands for "Priority/Reward Organizer," the No Nonsense people management key. A priority/reward organizer is someone who analyzes the potential rewards that will follow from the completion of a particular task, assigns a priority level to the task based on the reward, and completes high priority/high reward items first.

While this may sound quite reasonable for personal tasks and work assignments, it may sound cold and calculating when we urge you to follow it regarding family and friends. But it isn't. Think of P•R•O as a guide to help you organize all the things you *might* do so that you can devote your energies to the things you *should* and *want* to do.

What is a Priority?

A priority is something that comes ahead of other items because it is more urgent, important, or meritorious. Sometimes the priorities in a situation are obvious, sometimes not. To become a P•R•O, you must learn how to rank all of the items you must accomplish or wish to accomplish in their relative order of importance for completion.

Where to begin? You can't set priorities effectively unless you are clear about what you are trying to accomplish. And so we will begin, in the next chapter, with a discussion of *goals.*

2 · SETTING PERSONAL GOALS

Priorities and goals are the backbone of the P•R•O system. In order to establish priorities effectively you must understand how each particular task advances you toward one (or more) of your larger goals.

As we said in Chapter 1, you can't deal with others effectively until you understand yourself. So we will begin by discussing the process of setting personal goals. In Chapter 5 we'll move ahead to the process of setting mutual goals with others.

What Are Your Goals?

What are your goals? They may be objectives you are working toward actively right now, or they may be more distant. If you were to sit down and list the goals that seem important to you right now, perhaps the list would look something like this:

1. Get promoted to Supervisor.
2. Get a 10 percent per year raise.
3. Spend at least one full day each week with the family.
4. Spend two nights a week helping Brian with his homework.
5. Save $1,500 for Brian's college fund.
6. Exercise three times a week.
7. Save enough money for a two-week vacation for the family.

How Many Goals?

A person may have only one overriding goal—for example, the youngster who knows from an early age that being a doctor is his/her lifetime goal. We all know at least a few persons who have one overriding goal and can muster all their forces toward achieving it.

However, most of us are not that concentrated and have many goals. Often we have goals which suit us at a given time, but which change as we mature or move ahead.

Long-Term Goals

Long-term goals are those you want to accomplish over a period of many years. It is never too early or too late to think seriously about your long-term goals. Remember that the actual length of your long-term goals will vary depending on your age, health, etc. But no matter what your age or physical condition, establishing long-term goals is an essential part of managing your life.

Mid-Range and Short-Term Goals

Mid-range goals can be of two types—those that set you on the right course toward accomplishing your long-term objectives, and those that are independent goals themselves.

Your short-term goals are the most flexible and constantly changing of your goals. Exigencies of your job, family situations, or the burdens of daily life make your short-term goals a list that gets updated often, perhaps even daily.

Like mid-range goals, we prefer to think of short-term goals as having two components. The first are the constantly changing short-term items you have to do on an "as required by your daily life" basis. These include the report your boss needs by Friday at 5:00, shopping for toothpaste, preparing dinner for your relatives, etc.

The second component consists of those short-term objectives you need to reach in order to move toward your mid-range and long-term goals.

Changing Goals

Your goals may, and most likely will, change over time. Obviously, the child who wants to be a nurse at age eight may not stay with that ambition throughout life. For adults also, circumstances, chance, or rethought objectives can alter goals.

For this reason, we strongly recommend reanalyzing your goals periodically. How often is up to you. One of your authors takes a bit of quiet time each New Year's Day to rethink and reorganize longer-term goals. We recommend that you consider doing the same. And there is almost no limit to the number of times a year that you may find it profitable to rethink your mid-range and shorter-term goals.

Determining Personal Goals

Remember that before you can manage others, you must understand yourself. And since nothing is more important to you than your goals, you should treat the goal-setting process seriously.

Start with a clean sheet of paper, a pencil, and absolute quiet. Take all the time you need to think about what means the most to you and what you really want to accomplish during your life. What would you really like to be doing five, ten, or twenty years from now? Don't hide anything from yourself and don't hesitate to recognize your own desires, no matter how difficult or even impossible they may appear.

After taking the time you need, write your goals down. Note them briefly, without excessive verbiage, and as clearly as possible. Express your goals as much as possible in "action words" that stress what *you* can do.

Remember that goals are essentially personal. There are no "correct" goals, no right or wrong goals. Only you can determine what will make your life more satisfying and fulfilling.

An Example

Beth is a person who reevaluated her goals with excellent results. Beth studied special education in college, earning her degree with honors. She taught children with learning disabilities for many years, finding her job rewarding and satisfying. Her goal of being a teacher was fulfilled and fulfilling.

However, as the years passed, Beth began to feel stagnated in teaching. She realized that her interests and talents were more diversified and that she could help teenage girls in other ways than devoting herself to a classroom of perhaps twenty students.

Beth reevaluated and altered her long-term goals. She realized that she wanted the opportunity to be more creative. She discovered that she had a flair for and love of fashion. So, rather than concentrating on improving her teaching skills, Beth determined to become expert in buying and merchandising in the fashion field. She took courses in starting a small business and eventually achieved her new goal of owning and running a highly successful store specializing in clothes for preteen and teenage girls. Her old skills combined happily with the new. By rethinking her goals and rewards and prioritizing accordingly, Beth became a P•R•O.

3 · GOALS, REWARDS, AND PRIORITIES

We began Chapter 1 by urging you to become a P*R*O—a Priority/Reward Organizer. In Chapter 2, we encouraged you to think about your *goals* as an essential foundation for managing yourself, your time, and other people successfully. You are now ready to practice applying the P*R*O system to specific situations.

What is a Reward?

But first, what do we mean by reward? Obviously, every task or activity that we choose to do must carry some kind of reward, or we wouldn't do it. A reward can be anything you want or like. Rewards can be monetary—a raise or promotion to a better-paying job. They can be physical—the feeling of well-being after you complete a one-hour exercise program. Or they can be internal—a "job well done" by your boss, a "thank you" from a friend, or the knowledge that the completion of the task has moved you closer toward the accomplishment of your long-range goals. In short, a reward is anything you say it is—whatever pleases, gratifies, or satisfies you sufficiently so that you are motivated to complete a task or pursue an activity.

Establishing Priorities

To become a P*R*O, however, you must learn to distinguish carefully among rewards. Some rewards move you toward your long-term goals. Some rewards give you immediate gratification but have no further purpose. If you intend to reach your long-term goals, it is important not to let them be crowded out by immediate distractions.

We aren't saying that immediate rewards are unimportant, nor are we saying that they must necessarily conflict with longer-term goals. But where there *is* a conflict, keep your eye on your major goals. The tasks which go the farthest toward accomplishing your most important goals are the tasks you should establish as having the highest priority.

4 · ORGANIZING PRIORITIES

Now that you have taken time to think about your objectives and to set goals with the important people in your life, it is time to take the next step toward becoming a management P*R*O—understanding how to organize your priorities.

The Relationship Between Goals and Priorities

Your goals determine your priorities. Each task must be viewed as a step toward some goal. The tasks which go the furthest toward accomplishing your most important goals are the tasks you should establish as having the highest priority.

High Reward/High Priority

You can see that being a P*R*O requires that you constantly think and rethink your priorities. Before starting a task, you should analyze its reward potential. We suggest that you return to the list of goals you made in Chapter 2. Using that list, you will see that an item which carries a high potential reward in terms of moving you toward an important goal should be positioned on your P*R*O Scale as having a higher priority and should take up more of your time and effort than items with lower potential rewards.

By analyzing and organizing your priorities so that you work the hardest and the longest on items carrying the highest reward, you will also be constantly rethinking and redirecting yourself toward your goals.

"Do the Right Job—Not Just the Job Right"

Setting priorities can be difficult. You have to sort through many variables in order to prioritize properly. You must be sure to budget your time so that the most time is spent on tasks of highest priority. It is easy to make the error of spending too much time on the wrong project. One of our friends has a saying you should remember—"Do the right job, not just the job right."

You can only be effective when you do the right job well. Doing the wrong task well is ineffective, no matter how excellently that job is accomplished.

Priorities are Personal

Ultimately, of course, only you can decide what is the "right" job and what is not. Prioritizing is very personal. It is up to you to establish and change priorities according to your own goals and preferences. Only you can decide which tasks are most important to you and deserve the highest priority.

The strength of the P•R•O people management system is that it puts the maximum emphasis on your goals and your decisions. It forces you to look at tasks according to what *you* believe will give *you* the best rewards. By applying the P•R•O system, you will find yourself doing things because you *want* to, not because you *have* to. And even if the task is particularly distasteful to you, P•R•O will help you face it by concentrating on the reward you will receive when it is completed.

When Priorities Conflict

Setting priorities can often be complicated, especially when several legitimate goals and priorities conflict with each other. Thinking clearly and systematically about priorities won't make these conflicts go away, but it will make you better able to handle them.

As an example, let's say that your boss assigns the budget project for the next fiscal year to you. You have many other projects to work on, but you know that budgeting is an important part of a supervisor's position, and your Number One goal at work is to be promoted to supervisor. As a result, you must give the budget your highest work priority.

What happens when, in order to get everything done, you have to work late every night for two weeks and one full weekend in budget preparation? Another of your important goals is to help your son, Brian, with his homework at least two nights each week. You have directly conflicting goals, since it is impossible for you to work two nights per week with Brian and have the budget done on time.

What to do? If Brian is old enough, you may be able to explain to him how important this work project is to your chances of getting promoted, and how important the promotion would be for you and for the whole family.

But suppose Brian is too young to understand your rationale? And even if he understands the rationale, will his emotions not feel neglected? If, after careful thought, you decide that the budget must take precedence, your next priority must be finding a way to compensate Brian. Perhaps your spouse can give extra help with the homework for two weeks. And perhaps, in the two or three weeks after the budget project is completed, you could give up some purely personal pleasures in order to spend extra time with Brian.

Making Personal Choices

As we have said, setting priorities is a deeply personal matter, and different persons will choose their priorities differently. For example: Lois is a homemaker. While she has a master's degree in business administration, she has decided to devote the majority of her time to caring for her husband and two children. She works in a part-time job that allows her maximum flexibility so that she can easily take time off if her son has the flu or her daughter's scout group needs another chaperone for a field trip. Her priorities are at home, with her family.

Lois knows that she could earn more money if she were willing to work full time and to travel, but that is not what she wants right now. She has her education and is confident that she will be able to return to her profession full-time after her children are older.

Lois has set priorities that work for her.

Sandy, on the other hand, is very work oriented. She spends long hours on the job, often taking assignments home at night and working most weekends. Her two young children go to day care after school, and Sandy's substantial salary allows her to have live-in help to assist her at home and to care for the children while she works.

Sandy also has set priorities that work for her. Her priorities are different from Lois's, but each understands what is personally rewarding and how to structure her life to make those priorities paramount.

5 · SETTING GOALS TOGETHER

Setting goals for yourself and learning to prioritize will make you a P•R•O. However, in order to become a *Management* P•R•O, you must also set goals with those with whom you work and with family and friends.

The people you are close to can help you achieve your goals or they can get in your way. By articulating goals for yourself and setting mutual goals, you let those who are important to you understand what your primary desires are and how they fit into the larger picture of what must be done each day, week, and year. Or, to use a once-popular expression—it puts all of you "on the same wave length."

With Whom?

In order to be most effective, mutual goal setting should be done with your boss, associates, and subordinates at work, and also with family and friends.

Timing

We suggest that you set mutual goals with all of these individuals at least once each year. We do it just after New Year's. We also suggest that you update your mutual goal setting sometime during the year; around July 4 may work well.

Many people find more frequent updates helpful, finding that the additional sessions renew everyone's enthusiasm for achieving mutual goals and offering an occasion to reflect on past performance. Update sessions also have the advantage of providing time to air complaints or discuss criticisms.

Mutual Goals and Team Spirit

Studies indicate that people who feel that they are part of a team perform better, are more stable and happier. Mutual goal setting, whether at work or at home, makes everyone part of the team and gives all team members a stake in the success of the group.

At Work

A Management P•R•O sets goals with the people with whom he/she interacts at work. Goal setting need not be a time-consuming task, but it should be done thoughtfully and honestly.

Goals should be set with your boss, secretary, and subordinates. We will discuss dealing with each of these people in detail in Part IV. For now, let's simply discuss the goal-setting process.

How to Begin

As a Management P•R•O, it is up to you to initiate mutual goal setting. This applies to those who work for you and those for whom you work.

The first step is to make a list of all the people with whom you interact on a frequent basis on the job. The list obviously should include your boss, secretary, coworkers, and subordinates. But it could also include others who only tangentially impact your working life, such as the mail room clerk or housekeeper.

Next, take several sheets of paper and write the name of each person on your list on the top of a separate sheet. Then, on each sheet, write your goals for the next year vis-à-vis that person.

Your sheets might look like this:

Your Boss

1. Get promoted to division director.
2. Earn a $1,500 raise.

3. Become boss's right-hand person.

Your Secretary

1. Delegate more responsibility regarding correspondence.
2. Set up better telephone screening procedures.
3. Reorganize files.

Confer

The next step is to take your sheets and meet with the named person. This is the most important step in setting mutual goals—actually talking things out and deciding what's important.

The dialogue should be frank and constructive. It's important for both of you to understand your individual and mutual goals and how you plan to proceed.

Although this may sound simple and basic, it's amazing how often small problems are allowed to persist and worsen because of a failure to confer and communicate. For example, we know of an attorney who always complained that the housekeeping staff never cleaned his office properly. Trash that was on the floor one evening was still there the next day. After years of frustration, he sat down with the head housekeeper and really told him off. The housekeeper listened patiently and then explained to the lawyer that it is impossible for a cleaning person to know what is trash and what is valuable, and that if papers are strewn all over the floor, the housekeeping staff is instructed not to touch them, for fear of disturbing work in progress. The solution was obvious. The attorney began to throw his trash in the wastepaper basket and not haphazardly on the floor, and his office was cleaned to perfection from that day on.

With Your Boss

You may be hesitant to try to set goals with or for your boss, but you shouldn't be. Setting goals so that you understand what your boss expects and wants from you should improve your relationship and make your boss respect your approach to your work.

You can also help your boss understand your time problems, and incidentally recognize just how hard you have been working (in case you sometimes feel that he/she forgets), if you spend a short time periodically adjusting mutual goals.

And setting goals with your boss can be instructive. If two projects are due at approximately the same time and you don't know which your boss considers more important, a discussion may save you from wasting too much time working on the wrong one.

With Your Family and Friends

Families and friends have mutual goals, recognized or not, which underlie their relationship. These may be goals of nurturing (a child or elderly parent), mutual emotional support (a spouse or dear friend), or merely peaceful coexistence (a mother-in-law or teenage son).

One of our most popular short-term goals is to decide to see close friends and relatives at least twice during the next six months. By setting this as a goal, we feel doubly good when we make the social arrangements. First, we are happy to see our friends or relatives, and second, we have accomplished a goal.

Or, if you all feel that the family unit is disintegrating, you might set a mutual family goal of dining together once a week on some regular schedule, perhaps on Sunday evening.

By setting mutual goals with those with whom you live and/or work, you can better understand mutual priorities. This understanding of mutual priorities, in turn, can be a foundation for better cooperation and mutual respect.

PART II

P*R*O PLUS—RESPECTING SELF-ESTEEM

6 · COMMUNICATING AND LISTENING

Communicating and listening are the hallmarks of a Management P*R*O. By sharing valuable information, you gain insight, continue the mutual goal-setting process, and foster team spirit. But the most important thing about communicating with and listening to those with whom you work is that it means that you value their ideas enough to take the time to listen to them. This is the PLUS in P*R*O Management—respecting self-esteem.

Rules of Communication

There are times to get to the point and other times when "shooting the breeze" is appropriate. A Management P*R*O sets the parameters of communication so that the other person understands how to phrase his/her interruption or communication.

Consider the Time

At work, it is more likely that someone for whom or with whom you work will be engrossed in the business of the day and, unless there is a lull in activity, will not have the time to allot to irrelevant conversation. If you have such a lull and want to divert your mind and attention from your hard work by chatting with a coworker about sports or clothes, always ask the other person if this is a good moment for him/her to take time to chat. If the answer is no, suggest an alternative time, such as lunch.

Communication as a Means of Showing Respect

A Management P*R*O understands the time problems of others, communicates with them and values their self-esteem enough to respect their time and wishes.

Of course, the same is true at home. Here is an example. Peter works very hard every day at a job which demands his undivided and detailed attention. In the evening, he enjoys nothing more than a relaxing and chatty dinner with the family followed by an hour of quiet reading. He has set this quiet hour as one of their mutual goals and, because they respect Peter, they do not invade the hour unless an emergency intervenes.

The Management Listener

We all need to feel that what we have to say is valid. Studies have shown that infants want to be listened to when they babble or coo. It is the beginning of developing their sense of self-esteem and understanding that what they have to say is valuable.

Similarly, adults need recognition of their self-worth. If you interview people who work at menial or repetitive jobs, their major complaint will usually be that they know how to make things work better, but no one will listen to them. This is why the Japanese technique of "management circles" has been so productive and why Japanese workers feel that they are part of the production team and are respected. Self-respect leads to better job performance and greater productivity.

No Need to Listen to the Irrelevant

Of course, it is not necessary to listen to drivel. A Management P•R•O recognizes and understands how to direct a conversation toward productive ends, and gracefully concludes unproductive conversations.

Know What is Relevant

But just as parents listen intently when their baby babbles nonsense, so a Management P•R•O understands the point of allowing irrelevant conversation to foster camaraderie and exchange of ideas at the proper places. Some chief operating officers of major corporations spend at least one lunch hour each week dining in the employees' dining room, listening to workers and their complaints and suggestions. You have no idea how many great ideas have sprung from those seemingly wasteful conversations.

7 · HOW TO REWARD

The most important reward is the one that means the most to the recipient. If you have shared goals with those with whom you work and live, you will understand their aspirations and what they value as a reward.

Set Meaningful Rewards

One sure way of knowing what to use as a reward for the completion of a task is to set mutual rewards when the task is assigned.

For example, Ruth is the mother of four children. One of her family's mutual goals is for each child to keep his/her room neat and clean. When they set this goal, Ruth and the children also decided that each week all their rooms were neat and clean, they would go to the movies on Saturday. The children reasoned that each of them would police the others to ensure neatness so that all could be rewarded. So, every Friday, Ruth inspects the rooms and, if all are neat, everyone enjoys a treat.

We suggest you try this idea at work. When you set mutual goals with your boss or subordinates, we suggest that you also set rewards. How do you determine the nature of the reward? Ask. When you give someone an assignment, ask how the person wants to be rewarded. Make suggestions according to the difficulty of the task and the potential for outstanding performance.

One top lawyer we know rewards associate attorneys in his department for excellent performance by taking them to lunch at his private club. The feeling on the part of the associate being personally invited into the lawyer's private domain is the reward most sought after in that firm.

Another top manager we know thinks that a "job well done" or pat on the back is too fleeting a reward for a major effort, so she takes the time to handwrite a personal note to the employee expressing her thoughts on the excellent job. This note becomes a keepsake and can be shown to friends and family. This, she reasons, increases self-esteem at home, too.

Rewards Don't Have to be Monetary

But what of little rewards, of the nice things that keep everyone going through weeks and weeks of hard work? Have you ever sat down and asked yourself what you would most like as a reward after you complete a particularly time-consuming and difficult project? Now might be a good time to think about it. You will then be in a better position to understand how to reward those who work for you.

Studies have shown that barring a monetary or positional change, most workers want to know that their boss knows that they have done an excellent job. *They want communication, a reinforcement of their self-esteem.*

Pretty easy, isn't it? Well, unfortunately, most times the answer is no. How often has your boss actually called you into his/her office and said "great job"? We strongly recommend that all Management P•R•Os do this after a difficult assignment is completed. Too many people with power over others choose to exercise their power to provoke fear, only scolding and disciplining and never rewarding.

A Reward Doesn't Have to Take Long

You don't need to spend lots of time rewarding someone—but in order for the reward to be meaningful, it must be personal. Of course, there are times when it seems appropriate to publicly congratulate a worker, but in most cases, a more personal reward is preferable.

Rewards Must be Appropriate

The bottom line is that a reward is only rewarding if it is so to the recipient. The basic P•R•O PLUS concept is to communicate with those with whom you live, those for whom you work, and those who work for you, and this communication includes the process of setting mutual rewards. Obviously, it's better to give people rewards they want rather than rewards they don't want but that you think they should want.

Reward Yourself

And never forget that others aren't the only ones who can reward you. You can and should reward yourself for a job well done.

We find self-rewards especially important as a means of avoiding or ending procrastination. Promising yourself a specific reward may help you dive into that difficult or distasteful task you have been putting off. Make the reward substantial enough so that you feel positive about making the completion of the item a priority.

8 · HOW TO CRITICIZE

No one is always perfect, and the time occasionally comes for everyone to be told that his/her performance or behavior isn't satisfactory.

Criticize the Behavior, Not the Person

A Management P•R•O must always keep in mind the PLUS in the No Nonsense formula—respecting self-esteem. When you criticize, you don't want to attack or injure the person; you only want to eliminate unacceptable performance or behavior.

It is vitally important to remember that when dealing with a person whose job performance or love or friendship you value, the problem is not the person: the problem is with how the person has been performing.

Two Premises

You can see that we have established two premises for criticism. The first is that the person to be criticized is a worthy person. The second is that this worthwhile person has done something that is not up to his/her standards or potential.

At work, you must make the decision as to whether the person should continue in your employ. If the person to be criticized has the potential for excellent performance, or has performed well in the past, you will not want to throw away that potential hastily. Remember that it is costly to hire and train new personnel. And high employee turnover always has a negative effect on morale.

Putting the PLUS in Practice

We suggest that you always start any critique by remembering the PLUS and beginning with a statement that makes it clear that the person is basically "OK" to you. You might say, "I'd like to talk to you about the Harrison report,

Phil; it just wasn't up to your standards." Or, "This just isn't like you, Carolyn. You usually are so considerate of others."

Then talk about the problem at hand, be it poor behavior or poor job performance. The other person may try to offer an excuse, or may try to pass the blame onto others. You should listen for at least a while to the excuse; there may be some validity to it. But if the explanation or excuse is not adequate, you must assert your criticism. Whenever possible, make your case in positive terms of what the person should have done but did not do. For example: "If you were having a problem with Marvin's performance, you should have come to me and I would have helped. You can't use Marvin as an excuse."

The Critical Conclusion

Always try to end a critique with a positive note of encouragement. You might say, "I know you'll do better in the future; you have a lot of potential." Or, "This really isn't like you. I know you won't disappoint me again."

A positive ending to a criticism shows that you respect the other person and allows him/her to get back to work without embarrassment. By recognizing the individual's importance as a person, while saying that this particular job wasn't his/her best, you have encouraged the person to strive for greater achievement and perhaps also for a mutually selected reward discussed in Chapter 7.

Follow-up

You must be sure to follow up after a critique. If the person has to redo the assignment, you must be available to guide him/her so that the same or other mistakes won't be made again.

Don't Forget to Praise

Don't forget that it's obvious when someone has to be reprimanded, but it's equally important for a Management P*R*O to remember to give praise for a job well done.

PART III

THE ART OF DELEGATION

9 · WHY DELEGATE?

Delegating responsibility is a major step in becoming a Management P*R*O. You *can't* do everything yourself, no matter how efficient and intelligent you are. And, you *shouldn't* do everything yourself—the potential problems of "indispensability" both on a personal and a corporate level can be devastating, as we shall see below.

Newton Remembered

To paraphrase Newton—no two assignments can be done at the same time by the same person. In virtually every situation, one will and must take priority and precedence over the other.

It sometimes happens that you cannot do all the things you think you must do. Don't panic—be ruthless. The first step is to eliminate all unnecessary projects. The second step is to delegate to others every project that you can.

Delegation Is the Key to Managing

Webster's defines "manage" as "to control and direct; to . . . guide; administer." To be a manager, you must be able to delegate, because by delegating, you control and direct another person's time. It is said that a manager is only as effective as his/her ability to delegate, and that failure to delegate is failure to manage.

Indispensability

Many people feel that when they delegate their responsibility to someone else, they are somehow diminishing their value to the organization. Actually, nothing could be further from the truth. The consequence of not delegating is the condition of "indispensability," which creates a bottleneck of inefficiency.

Many people who are proud of being indispensable believe that it assures job security and longevity. After all, they reason, an indispensable person can't be fired or laid off, since no one else knows how to do his/her job. Right? Wrong. The reality is that indispensability leads to multilevel stagnation.

The first level of stagnation is a personal one. If only you can do a particular task, then that task always has to be done by you. After you do it over and over, you will surely get bored and find your job less stimulating and rewarding. You will not grow in your job and will not be available to assume new responsibilities, and your selfishness in not training others will be perceived as a lack of management skills. On a corporate level, your indispensability affects those working under you. They cannot advance, because you have not trained them to assume your job once you move on to bigger and better things.

Delegation as Personal Growth

So delegation leads to growth, both for the person delegating and for the one delegated to. Delegation doesn't mean that you no longer *can* do a particular job, but rather that you no longer *choose* to do certain jobs, and that your expertise allows you to supervise others in attaining your level of competence. By training others to grow into your job, delegation frees you to spend time on more challenging and demanding assignments.

Delegation Is Not Abdication of Responsibility

When you delegate an assignment to another, you are not "passing the buck" to him/her. Rather you are taking on the additional responsibility of supervising the delegated performance in addition to doing your own tasks. This is the essence of good management.

Follow Up

While delegation frees you to assume new responsibilities, it does not totally relieve you of your old duties. This is where P*R*O PLUS comes to bear. Remember the self-esteem of the person to whom you have delegated. Follow up with him/her to make sure that the task is being properly accomplished. Be available at regular times for consultation, and don't let things go for long in a wrong direction. If you must criticize, do so in a way that respects self-esteem and leads to growth, not anger.

But Encourage Independence

On the other hand, a manager should not be too ready with answers. This can foster overdependence by subordinates, defeating the very purpose of delegation. Be wary of saying, "Don't do anything without first checking with me," an attitude which will make your staff become too dependent. You must allow for mistakes as a result of delegation. Your principal concern is to make sure that the same mistakes don't happen more than once.

You must also be wary of getting bogged down in trivial detail. Once you have delegated an item, the person to whom you have delegated may want to tell you in great detail about everything he/she has done. This is clearly a time waster, and you must state that you want and need to hear only the essentials; do so in a way that stresses your confidence in the person, rather than your need not to be bothered. Keep in mind that if you wanted to know all the details, you would have done the job yourself.

You Are Ultimately Responsible

Even though you have delegated a task to someone else, you are ultimately responsible for its completion. This is true whether you are the owner of a company or an employee. That is why it is so important to communicate clearly when delegating assignments. We will discuss *how* to delegate in the next chapter.

Delegation as a Mutual Goal

Finally, remember delegation when you are setting mutual goals, since few mutual goals are more important or more productive. Remember what we said earlier, that delegation means progress for both the superior and the subordinate. Delegation is an essential part of the process of education and growth, at home as well as at work. It is important for the young child who wants to learn to cook, just as it is important for the worker who wants to understand the budgeting process, or the young attorney who wants to learn how to prepare an effective appellate brief.

10 · HOW TO DELEGATE

Knowing when and how to delegate, and to whom, is critical to being a good manager.

When to Delegate

As a rule, you should delegate as much of your work as possible. Routine tasks should always be delegated. Be wary of the sometimes uncontrollable desire to become involved in every step of an operation. Total involvement may give you an ego-boosting feeling of importance, but it is a serious management time waster.

Delegate According to Priority

Low priority/low reward items, including routine tasks, should always be delegated.

High priority/low reward items should similarly be delegated, because your valuable time should not be spent on items with a low P•R•O scale reward quotient. However, these high priority/low reward items should merit your special review because of their high priority nature.

Low priority/high reward items may be delegated and personally reviewed, or you may reserve them to do yourself at a later date when their priority is greater.

High priority/high reward items deserve your personal attention and should rarely be delegated.

To Whom?

Because delegating is a learning and training experience, you should consider delegating to the person with the lowest ability or training who can qualify to handle the task.

How to Delegate

Gypsy Rose Lee is credited with having said; "Anything worth doing well is worth doing slowly." That is certainly true of delegation.

You must delegate slowly and carefully. Clearly detail the responsibilities delegated and your goals for completion. Tell the person why you have chosen him/her for this assignment and try to motivate as you delegate. To assure good communication, ask the person to restate your instructions, and especially the timetable for completion. And don't forget to follow up.

Delegate Early

To delegate successfully, it is important that you delegate items as soon as possible. The person to whom you delegate very likely will not be able to do the task as quickly as you would yourself. Moreover, you need ample time to review the results and to reinstruct the person on improving parts of the assignment that are still not up to standard. The more time you can allow for this process, the better for everyone.

The executive who fails to delegate successfully is likely to act something like this:

The task comes to the executive's desk. Since the deadline isn't immediate, the executive is "too busy to think about it," or even to decide whether to delegate it or not. The next time the executive rummages through his/her desk and encounters the item, there is no doubt that it had better be delegated, but the executive is "too busy to take time to explain it to someone."

Finally, when the deadline is imminent, the executive may do the task himself/herself out of desperation; delegate it improperly, that is, to someone with expertise who is also under tremendous time pressures; or delegate it properly, to a less experienced individual, but with a hasty explanation and little discussion. In the latter two situations, it is almost impossible for the subordinate to perform adequately, and the executive ends up fuming that the job was done poorly or not on time.

Think About Assignments

Even some high priority/high payoff items can be delegated to a certain degree. Let's say your boss asks you to prepare the annual salary analysis and job description report. This is a high priority "hands on" project and you must see that it is done properly.

Break It Down

Does that mean that you must handle every detail? Of course not. You should break down the report process into its component parts. You will need a great deal of information. You can assign one person to do all of the many tasks and write a preliminary draft, or you can assign various people to different parts of the report, with you or someone else doing the preliminary assembling.

An Example

Lauri is a recent law school graduate working in a major law firm. She has a good education, but almost no practical experience. Her immediate boss, Donald, is a sixth-year associate who hopes to be made a partner of the firm at the end of the year. His boss, Frances, is the head partner of the litigation department. Frances assigns a new and important piece of litigation to Donald, indicating that this litigation, if handled properly, could result in his becoming a partner. The litigation involves many questions of law in the area of trade secrets, with which Donald has some expertise. Lauri is eager to learn, but has no particular expertise.

The key for Frances is getting the matter done and done well. She assigns Donald to the case because she knows that he is competent and understands trade secrets. The client involved is a major one, the case is important, and she can't afford any mistakes. She clearly communicates that fact to Donald.

Donald has many other matters he is currently handling. He explains that to Frances, who understands his dilemma but reiterates that this new matter must be added to his already crowded case load. Donald recognizes the importance of the case to him in terms of his desired partnership, his highest possible reward. Considering Lauri to be bright and energetic, he suggests that she assist him in the matter. Frances agrees, and Lauri is brought into the meeting. The importance of the client is explained to her and the details of the case are discussed.

What has just happened represents P•R•O PLUS in action, combining excellent initial communication, mutual goal setting and delegation of responsibility. All parties understand the priority which must be given to the new matter. Frances's reward will be monetary and a greater division of partnership profits if the case is handled well. Donald's dream of becoming a partner could become a reality. And Lauri, who has just joined the firm, has her first chance to show her ability and become a member of the team.

Now that rewards and priorities have been mutually agreed upon, it is time for work to begin. Donald and Lauri go through the file together. They determine exactly what has to be done and in what order. They establish a calendar with due dates for completion of certain tasks. Donald includes Lauri's due dates on his own calendar so that he can follow her progress periodically. See Chapter 15.

Frances also marks her calendar with the due dates and periodically checks with Donald for a progress report. Donald and Lauri meet frequently to check on Lauri's progress. The result? Frances has time to pursue more clients and to devote herself to several of the more complicated and sophisticated matters in the office. Donald will continue to handle his crowded case load and will handle the more complicated parts of the new case himself, while Lauri will get her feet wet on the less complicated items in the new matter. Donald's overburdened schedule is slightly reduced; Lauri has a valuable learning experience in which she has the advantage of working with other attorneys who are more experienced.

PART IV

DEALING WITH . . .

11 · YOU AND YOUR SECRETARY

A boss and secretary are a team. Their relationship should be one of trust and mutual understanding. It is estimated that a good secretary can *double* a manager's efficiency.

In order for the boss/secretary team to function, mutual goals and objectives must be established and rewards understood. Communication is the key.

Write a Job Description

Responsibilities must be articulated; they cannot be assumed. One good way to ensure mutual understanding of responsibilities is to sit down with your secretary and write a job description with him/her. Some bosses and secretaries prefer individually to write the secretary's job description and then compare their lists. Either way, you will find this an excellent way of communicating and organizing procedures.

The following paragraphs describe some items you might consider including in your secretary's job description.

The Telephone and Visitors

Develop a telephone screening system and a time each day for your secretary to schedule return calls and/or visits. Instruct your secretary to delegate certain types of calls to others in the office. Give him/her a list of those people whose calls you will take no matter what (including, for example, your spouse, children, boss, the President of the United States, etc.). And, make sure that your secretary's desk is strategically located so that all visitors encounter him/her before you come into view.

Your Calendar

Your secretary should be familiar with and have access to your calendar. Teach him/her any idiosyncratic systems you have developed. Instruct your secretary about the types of appointments and meetings he/she can set up for you. Establish a method whereby your secretary informs you of items he/she has scheduled and any changes that have been made.

Dictation

Do you dictate in person or to a tape? Do you or your secretary have a preference? Tape has the advantages of saving a secretary's time and of allowing you to dictate when your secretary is unavailable. If you dictate in person, establish a time each day for handling dictation and reviewing the typed product. Establish a system for handling "emergency" dictation.

Mail

Teach your secretary to screen your mail, discarding irrelevant paper and organizing the remainder for easy handling by you. Indicate what is to be done with "confidential" or "personal" correspondence—should your secretary open it or not? He/she will not know, unless you make it clear.

Also, set up procedures for handling the mail you have reviewed each day—what is to be filed, what delegated to others, etc.

Take Your Secretary Into Your Confidence

If your team is to work efficiently, your secretary must know and understand your work projects and priorities. If you can't trust your secretary to be discreet, then hire a new secretary.

Listen to Your Secretary

Let your secretary be your eyes and ears. He/she will hear more about you and the company than you will. If your secretary makes suggestions, listen and consider them carefully. Always encourage dialogue with your secretary; he/she may have constructive thoughts regarding your time and productivity.

Encourage Questions

Always encourage your secretary to ask questions. If he/she doesn't understand something, the chances are that others will be confused as well.

Encourage Greater Responsibility

Always encourage your secretary to assume greater responsibility, take initiative, use his/her judgment, anticipate problems, and screen irrelevancies. This will allow him/her to grow in the job and will relieve you of unnecessary details.

Meetings

Your secretary should be present at all meetings you schedule. While he/she probably will not participate in the meeting, he/she will take and distribute the minutes and schedule subsequent meetings.

Discuss Rewards

At least once a year, you and your secretary should have a discussion about rewards. Find out what his/her expectations are for the next year. Don't let embarrassment hinder an open and frank discussion.

Meet Regularly

Periodic meetings with your secretary will ensure that your priorities are established and that you mutually understand both your priorities and the potential rewards. On a more immediate level, many bosses and secretaries have a meeting every day, for a brief period, to go over the daily agenda and to plan ahead. This is a very helpful and valuable P*R*O planning tool. Not only does it keep both of you on the right track, but it reinforces your secretary's self-esteem (the PLUS) by including him/her in the important events of your day.

Yes, You Can Begin Again

What happens if you and your secretary have been working together reasonably well, but one or both of you would like to change certain elements of the situation? The solution is P*R*O PLUS communication.

Set aside time for a meeting when you can both talk about your goals, procedures, and rewards. If you haven't ever done this in the past, you might take the opportunity to explain the P*R*O PLUS system and tell your secretary that you want to begin to implement it. Work on a job description together, and be clear about the duties and responsibilities you expect your secretary to fulfill.

Praise and Appreciation

Finally, don't fall into the trap of only mentioning things that are wrong. Let your secretary know when things are going well. For example, if your secretary's letters are always perfect and elegant-looking, remember periodically to say thank you. If he/she is very considerate of your needs, doing little things to help you through crises and traumas, do something nice in return.

Remember, your secretary can make your life a lot easier. Try to make your secretary's life easier as well.

12 · YOU AND YOUR BOSS

"Managing" your boss—it's an interesting and perhaps frightening thought. But we assure you that the P*R*O PLUS system can be applied to your boss as well as to subordinates.

It is essential that you understand your boss's expectations of you and your work. One of the best ways to do this is to set goals together (Chapter 5). And, when you set goals, you also should establish rewards.

Setting Goals and Rewards Together

Mutual goal and reward setting doesn't have to be overly time consuming. It can take as little as a minute or two. Or you both may find that a fuller discussion is needed.

When your boss assigns a new project to you, ask immediately about the relative importance of the new project vis-à-vis your other assignments. If your boss tells you to give the new project the highest priority, ask immediately about your other projects—they also have due dates that may not be met if priority is given to this new assignment. You and your boss will then have to consider and reevaluate all your priorities. Mutual goal setting will give you direction and prevent you from concentrating your energies in the wrong direction.

Prepare for the Discussion

Let's look at the process in more detail. We'll assume that assignments have already been prioritized with your boss according to P*R*O importance. Now an additional assignment has been given to you—how do you handle it?

We suggest that when your boss is ready to meet with you, you take with you a list of all the matters on which you are currently working and those awaiting your attention. You will then have no trouble telling your boss about your current projects and discussing how the new task fits into the list.

Always redo your priorities with your boss whenever a new project is assigned. This will help you avoid the panicky and overwhelmed feeling that is all too common when you have too much to do and not enough time in which to do it.

Speak Up Now

Don't wait until it is too late to speak up about conflicting and/or overwhelming priorities. Once you begin a project, or let any substantial time elapse between the assignment and beginning the project, you have used valuable time that another person might have applied to the assignment.

Handling Revisions on Your Own

The best way to avoid backlogs and bottlenecks is to share your goals and plan mutually with your boss. If it isn't possible for you to confer with him/her when a new assignment arises, make a reasonable priority decision on your own and write a brief memo to your boss stating your revised priorities. The memo need not be elaborate, but it should include your reasons for the new order of priorities you have established. Then, even if you have made some error of judgment, your reasons are on the record, your credibility is intact, and your boss can come back to you with suggested changes if he/she so desires.

13 · YOU AND YOUR SUBORDINATES

We have treated your secretary separately from other subordinates because of the special relationship between boss and secretary. Dealing with other subordinates is somewhat different, since the working relationship is usually less close.

Why the Buddy System Doesn't Work

You can operate a family like a business, but you cannot run a business like a family. It follows from this that the "buddy system" of dealing with subordinates invariably doesn't work. No matter how interested you are in the lives of those with whom you work, and no matter how caring and considerate you are, there is still the inescapable fact that one person is the boss and is responsible for giving direction to the others. If you are too much of a buddy and not enough of a boss, it becomes increasingly difficult to criticize subordinates effectively and to evaluate their performance objectively.

Communicate

As with other people with whom you work, we suggest frequent communication with your subordinates. Your communications can be in person or in writing, or a combination of the two.

It is remarkable how much loyalty and good will can be generated if you take the time to communicate with your subordinates about your work plans and their participation as part of your team. This doesn't mean that you must necessarily reveal your personal hopes and aspirations to your subordinates; but communicating your broad general plans and your thoughts as to how your subordinates fit into the plan will always be most helpful.

Set Mutual Goals

By now, you know that a Management P•R•O sets mutual goals with those for whom and with whom he/she works. It is a good idea to set goals with subordinates on a regular basis. For example, some P•R•Os set goals quarterly, evaluating performance and objectives at the same time, using the PLUS system.

We heartily recommend frequent reevaluation, which lets both bosses and subordinates communicate and express problems. Try not to let these become criticism sessions. Try to make them constructive, emphasizing the good work that has been done as well as the problems.

Be a Role Model

In your position as a boss, it is important for you to be a good role model. You must be efficient and use your time wisely, so that you will be a person to emulate. See Part V.

Recognize the Burdens of Subordinates

Over and over again, studies have shown that people are happier and more productive in their jobs if they believe that the work they are doing is challenging, creative, and manageable. The question as to what is "manageable" may be complicated, since these same studies show that most people like to feel that they have just a bit too much to do. This feeling keeps them moving and on their toes.

But you can't be a slave driver. You must listen if a subordinate tells you that completing a task by the date you have set is simply not possible. You must then consider whether your assignments have been too burdensome or whether the subordinate is just not up to the challenge.

Turnovers Mean Waste

It costs money to lose employees. New people have to be interviewed, trained, and oriented. Time has to be spent integrating them into the operation—and time is money and productivity. So a Management P•R•O understands that it is important to keep a valuable subordinate happy as well as busy.

Delegate with Challenge

When you delegate a task to a subordinate, try to phrase the assignment as a challenge. Always encourage and assist a subordinate. Remember his/her self-esteem.

Open Door Policy

Many managers feel that they should keep their office doors open to encourage communication. But more often than not, this only wastes time. An open door is a signal that you are totally available and that anyone who wants to or needs to can come right in. This is rarely productive. As a boss, you need to make sure that others value your time and recognize that unnecessary interruptions will keep you from accomplishing your tasks.

You may have certain hours each day when you choose to keep your door open and let your subordinates know that you are available for their important questions and problems. Remember, however, that a total open door policy is invariably counterproductive.

14 · YOU AND YOUR FAMILY AND FRIENDS

It is often more difficult to deal with those with whom you are close—your family and friends—than with those with whom you work. There is, of course, a difference in the quality of family and work relationships. A professional relationship is usually unidimensional and is not intended to impinge on the personal side of life. We expect that family and friendship relationships will be fuller, richer, and many-sided.

Communicate

At home as on the job, the first rule is—talk things over. Set mutual goals and work toward making them a reality. Understand how your family and friends want to be treated, what they consider appropriate rewards, and act accordingly.

Exercising Authority

In a family relationship, there will be times when a parent has to tell a child to do something because it is necessary for the good of the child or the family. Democracy takes second place to other needs. But in most cases, nothing is more important than growth and mutual responsibility, and communication is the key.

Criticize the Deed, Not the Person

At home, just as on the job, there may be times when you recognize a need to criticize. But when you are dealing with family and friends, even more than on the job, it is necessary to emphasize that while a certain action may deserve criticism, the person is someone you love or care for. This may sound obvious, but it is surprising how many long-lasting family feuds have resulted from a critical comment poorly taken.

So think carefully before you criticize, and consider how to make your criticism acceptable and constructive. Remember that while you may not work with the same people all of your life, your friends, and even more your relatives, are forever.

When you criticize, do so with care and affection.

Keep in Touch

Another frequent source of friction in families and between friends is the failure of one person to keep in touch. You don't have to take long on the telephone to show that you care—but a phone call every once in a while to certain relatives and friends is certainly a good idea. If you tend to forget, jot down a reminder on your calendar (see Chapter 15) until it becomes a habit.

PART V

MANAGING YOURSELF

15 · GETTING ORGANIZED—CALENDARS AND LISTS

A P*R*O must be able to organize priorities and time effectively. Once you have established and organized your goals and priorities, you must have a system of time management to assure completion. For a more complete discussion of time management, we suggest that you read the No Nonsense Career Guide, *How To Use Your Time Wisely*. But here we will briefly discuss some of the essentials.

Introducing Calendars

Your calendar is the clearing house for the management of your time and priorities. Calendars help you plan for occasions, note when certain tasks have to be finished, and organize your game plan. Use your calendar as an extension of your memory. Write down appointments, things to do, and ideas to remember. Once you determine what must be done, write the due dates on your calendar.

Master Calendar

While we recommend the use of two calendars, a master and a portable one, the master calendar is by far the more important. Everyone who hopes to organize his/her time and priorities should keep a master calendar. On this calendar is registered each appointment as well as goals for the day, week, and/or month.

A calendar with lots of writing space for each day is ideal. We prefer the type that is desk size and presents a week at a time. This allows you to see what you have scheduled for the week and what time you have available to allocate.

Portable Calendar

For those who do not work at home, a portable calendar for the pocket or purse is indispensable. While you don't have to put every item from your master calendar on your portable calendar, all actual appointments, meetings, etc., should be recorded in both places. Some people now use pocket-size computers as portable calendars; they can be programmed to list meetings, appointments, opera tickets, dress and shoe sizes, etc.

Secretary's Calendar

People with secretaries usually find it helpful for their secretary or assistant to keep a corresponding master calendar (usually including only work-related appointments and events) so that the secretary/assistant can be aware of activities and help meet your scheduling demands.

Check In with Your Calendar

Make a habit of checking your calendar the first thing every morning, or just before you go to bed. Some people find it helpful to go over their next day's schedule just before they retire—they claim that their subconscious begins to work out problems while they are asleep. We cautiously suggest that you give this a try, especially if there are pressing problems you can't seem to solve during the day.

Plan Your Year

You should prepare your master calendar at the beginning of each year. Write all of your periodically recurring events on the calendar. These include filing your income tax return on April 15; filing quarterly tax estimates in April, June, September, and the following January; regular dentist and doctor appointments; paying the rent or mortgage on the first of every month; etc.

Organize with Lists

How can you remember the things you have to do, the things you want to do, and your goals, while at the same time coping with everyday life? Unless you have a perfect memory, which few of us have, there is only one efficient way—set your priorities and then make lists.

Monthly List

You should reevaluate your handling of priorities on a regular basis. A good idea is to take 15 minutes the first of every month to analyze what you have accomplished toward your goals in the last month and what you hope to do this month.

You may want to make a monthly list only for a few months until you become better organized and goal oriented, or you may find the monthly reevaluation of your goals too useful to eliminate. How often you rethink your lists is partly a matter of personal preference. But for a start, keeping your priorities and goals in mind, look at the coming month and see what you can accomplish during it to advance your objectives.

The Essential Daily List

Your daily "to do" list is an essential. It is begun from your calendar. Obviously your long-range goals aren't the only priorities you have to think about each day. There are daily job and family responsibilities as well as the necessities of living, such as doing the laundry and shopping for groceries.

A daily list helps you avoid the terrible feeling that you have wasted most of the day. And since the list is freshly organized each day, you can always revise it in case of an emergency.

Making the List Efficient

Some people prefer to organize their daily list the first thing in the morning. Others do it the night before. But don't neglect making the list, and don't trust your memory. The daily list has to be written down, on a piece of paper small enough for you to carry for reference throughout the day.

Try to be specific and break each item into its component parts. Don't list "make phone calls." Rather list

1. Return Robyn's call.
2. Call Sam.
3. Call Celestine.
4. Buy birthday card for Pat.

Be Realistic

Try not to overschedule yourself each day. You should arrange your items by priority and add a second lower priority list, just in case you have some time. For example, if you need toothpaste and deodorant, you might have a separate "drug store" list. If you find yourself near a drug store, you could run in and buy the items on your list for a bonus accomplishment that day.

16 · DEALING WITH PAPER

P•R•O management extends not only to people but also to inanimate items that limit productivity. There is no better example than the time-consuming mass of paper we generate and receive each day.

Studies have shown that the reason papers pile up is that the recipient of the paper either can't or won't decide what to do with it. This holds true for mail we receive, newspapers and magazines we buy, and paper we generate. It is important to do something with each piece of paper. Never just put a piece of paper down. Always make some decision about it.

Three Choices

We have developed three No Nonsense choices for coping with paper at work and at home. They are:

Toss It!
File It!
Move It!

Toss It!

At least 80 percent of the paper you encounter can be tossed into the trash without ceremony. Be brutal. Most paper is unnecessary, unwanted, and without merit. If you don't need it, don't want to file it, and have no one to give it to—toss it in the trash.

File It!

Much of the mail you get in the office, and some of the mail you get at home, should be filed for further reference. We will talk about setting up a home filing system in Chapter 17.

But most of what you receive can be read and tossed. If you don't think you will ever need the piece of paper in the future—don't file it—toss it.

Move It!

This is perhaps our most difficult rule. If the piece of paper represents something that someone else can handle with greater knowledge or efficiency, delegate it and move it to him/her. And don't forget that delegating responsibility extends to the home as well as the workplace.

The Dots Have It

As an experiment, we'd like you to take this famous time management test.

Every time you receive a piece of paper, put a small dot in the upper right corner of the paper. Then every time you handle that piece of paper again, add one more dot. When you have five dots, you *must* do something with the paper. You will be surprised how quickly the dots accumulate and how many times you waste precious seconds handling and rehandling the same paper. Our three-choice rule will save you from this waste of time.

Consolidate Efforts

Try to put all similar papers together and deal with them at once. If you gather all the letters you must answer, you can respond to all of them when you are in a letter-writing mood.

With a Secretary

If you are fortunate enough to have a secretary, one of his/her daily jobs can be to pre-sort your mail. You should instruct him/her to divide mail into three categories—items marked personal or confidential which you are to receive unopened, junk mail for your quick perusal and tossing (these can be tossed by your secretary, if you wish), and items which have to be acted upon.

There may be correspondence or other matters that your secretary can handle without your input. For example, letters that get a form reply can be answered and the letter and reply can be presented to you for signature.

If there is a request for a meeting, your secretary can tentatively determine the time and then confirm it with you later, noting it on your calendar.

All mail that you can move gets returned to your secretary immediately for rerouting. You may want to make a note on the top of the page addressed to the next recipient, indicating the action you want taken. This informal notation will save your secretary's time, since no memo is required. Of course, there will be times when you need to move a piece of paper with lengthy instructions. In that case, put the paper in your "today" file for completion (see Chapter 17). And remember—before you put it aside, put a dot at the top.

Without a Secretary

The only difference in dealing with the mail when you don't have a secretary is that you have to open and sort the correspondence yourself.

Try to be ruthless. Use dots. Move it, file it, or toss it. The more efficient you are and the more you get done, the more likely it is that you will one day have a secretary to help you.

Paper At Home

Now let's consider the surprising amount of paperwork you must deal with at home. We suggest that every homemaker have a desk—a place where all paperwork can be handled. The desk should be near your files and easily accessible to a telephone. In that way paperwork, correspondence, phone calls, and the calendar can be handled at one convenient location.

Let's begin with paper we order.

Magazines

Here are several No Nonsense tips about magazines: (1) If you haven't read the magazine in the last six months—don't renew the subscription. (2) Before you renew a subscription, list three good reasons why you want this magazine. If you can't list three, don't renew. (3) When you first receive any magazine, skim it to determine which articles you want to read. If you commute to work, or have bits of wasted time waiting in lines, etc., tear out the article and put it in your reading file. See Chapter 17. (4) If you haven't finished the magazine before the next one arrives, go through the magazine, tear out the articles that are important to you, put them in your reading file, and toss the rest.

Newspapers

Newspapers can accumulate, and an old newspaper has very little value except as kindling for a fire.

Never accumulate newspapers. *Never.* Read what is essential and timely in the newspaper each day. Try not to get bogged down reading irrelevant articles. It is better to clip what you want to read and put it in your reading file. See Chapter 17.

Be brutal—newspapers take up space, create a fire hazard, prey on your mind, and produce a feeling of general disorganization that is not conducive to productivity or good time management.

Mail

We get more letters every year—and rarely do they involve correspondence we have initiated. At home, we get catalogues, direct mail solicitations, junk, offers that seem (and usually are) too good to be true, bills, important correspondence, and more junk. The three No Nonsense paper handling rules must be brutally applied to this mail and it should be tossed, filed, or moved immediately to another family member who can handle it more efficiently.

Notices and Engagements

Notices of meetings you want to attend or engagements you have made need to be noted immediately on your personal calendar, your master calendar, and those of your spouse or guest, if you are taking one to the event.

17 · FILING

Files are an essential part of organization. They are therefore a necessity for a Management P•R•O. A filing system provides easy access to all the pieces of paper you need to keep.

A filing system should be intelligible to you and to others. Files should usually be arranged alphabetically and cross-referenced for easy access. Additions to files should be uniformly placed either at the front or the back of the individual file folder.

How Many Files?

The first rule is to set up adequate files. If you do the job right, you will probably find that you need more file drawers and more folders than you originally guessed. But it's much better to have too many files (they can always be eliminated) than to let paper accumulate because you don't have the proper place to put it.

Tickler Files

Tickler files remind you to do things in the future. You use a tickler file to store documents that must be handled at a later date, or to hold reminders of future events. Your tickler file works in tandem with your calendar. Your calendar shows meetings and other events. The paperwork for these meetings and other backup reminders should be placed in your tickler files. We find it most convenient to keep tickler files handy in our desk.

There are two basic types of tickler files. We recommend using both in combination.

Monthly Tickler

The first is a monthly tickler file. This is a divided file that has 12 compartments, one for each month of the year.

When an item comes up that has to be handled in a future month, you put a note to that effect in the appropriate compartment.

For example, say that you have an annual physical every November. You put a note "annual physical" in the November compartment, and once you have completed your current physical, you replace the note for the following November. A recurring item, such as an annual physical, should also be listed on your calendar.

Let's take another example. Suppose your boss wants you to check with him/her in two months regarding the progress of a specific account. As you gather information in the interim, you file it in the appropriate month's compartment in preparation for your report. Should your boss forget, your tickler file will alert you to remind him/her.

Daily Tickler

The second type of tickler file is a daily file. This has 31 compartments, one for each day of the month. Used in combination with a monthly file, your efficiency will soar.

When the first day of each month comes along, all the information and papers should be taken out of that month's tickler file and placed in the appropriate places in your daily tickler file. You should also double check to make sure that any meetings or other relevant dates are noted on your calendar.

You "trace" items up to the appropriate day. Let's say that you need a report from Sam on June 12. You tell Sam about the report on June 1. Knowing how busy Sam is, it seems wise to remind him about the report to make sure that he is working on it. So you trace it up to the sixth, by dropping a note about Sam's report in your compartment marked "6." On the sixth, you give Sam a call, or drop him a memo about the report. Then, on the twelfth, you take the "Sam reminder" out of your file, and—hopefully—his report will be ready.

This is an excellent system to use both in the office and at home. You should check the appropriate section of your daily tickler file each morning just after you check your calendar. The items in today's section go immediately into your "today" file.

Specialized Files

In addition to standard alphabetical files and a tickler system, we find that a number of specialized files can be of help. These include files labeled "today," "work in progress," "project," named files for family, subordinates, and superiors, a "mail" file, and "reading" files.

Today File

Let's begin with a file we have already discussed, the "today" file. The "today" file contains all the important documents and other items that must be handled within the next 24 hours. Many secretaries prepare a daily agenda for their boss as the first page in the "today" file.

All of the items that need immediate attention, plus the output from your daily tickler compartment, should be put in this file. The "today" file is a transient file. Once the item is handled, it is removed from the "today" file and either filed, tossed or moved.

Remember that anything to be accomplished today should be put in your "today" file—whether it is the file on the meeting regarding your most important client, or as mundane as the dry cleaning slips to remind you that you are out of clean shirts.

"Work in Progress" File

Items that you are working on currently, but that are not due today, should be put in a "work in progress" file. You should review this file at least weekly, and perhaps even daily, to be sure you are aware of all uncompleted items; and you should tie in the "work in progress" file with your daily tickler by putting reminder notes in the tickler for each approaching "work in progress" deadline.

Superior/Subordinate Files

You should have a file for each person to whom you report and for each person who reports to you. This can include family members.

Mail File

If you have a secretary or assistant, you will probably want to have a "mail" file in which the day's correspondence is placed. As you go through the mail, certain items may be put in your tickler file, or there may be an urgent item that belongs in your "today" file. The remaining items that must be moved to another person can be returned in the "mail" file to your secretary for distribution.

Meeting Files

Some people prefer not to include documents required for meetings in their "today" file, but instead have a "meeting" file for that purpose. Others use separate files for each meeting they must attend. We suggest that you put a note in each meeting file listing the separate project files you will want to bring to that meeting.

Reading File

A "reading" file is the place where you put all the articles and other items you want to read after clipping them out of the magazine or newspaper (and throwing out the rest). You can take out your "reading" file during your less productive hours, or you can take it with you when you anticipate a waiting or traveling period. Some prefer to take selected items from their "reading" file and fold them in their pocket or purse to take out while waiting in the supermarket checkout line. Others prefer to take the entire file and select articles on the spot.

18 · COPING WITH INTERRUPTIONS

Part of being a P*R*O is to be in control of your time. This chapter deals with maintaining control when the unexpected happens.

An interruption is a divergence from the day you have planned. It may be a welcome break, such as a phone call from an old friend, or an unwelcome one. What is important is how you deal with the interruption.

Because interruptions are unexpected, they have to be handled on the spot. You must make a quick decision regarding the best use of your time. Your decision will depend on a number of things including what you are doing at the time, what you have scheduled for the day, and the length and importance of the interruption.

Be Honest

It is essential to be honest about your priorities. You must take your priorities seriously and you must explain them clearly to others, if you expect others to take them seriously and respect them.

The Telephone

Not all interruptions are unexpected. Your father may call you every day between 9:00 and 9:30 A.M. That is an interruption, but not an unexpected one. If that time becomes inconvenient for you, simply tell him that from now on, you would prefer it if he would phone between 10:00 and 10:30. An easy solution.

But what of unexpected calls? Our answer must be divided into two—one for those of us who have a secretary, and one for those who do not.

Your Secretary as First Line of Defense

Your secretary can solve 90 percent of your telephone problems and make the telephone work for you instead of against you. He/she can screen your calls, protect you from unnecessary interruptions when you are in a high priority/high productivity mode, tell callers when to phone to meet your convenience, and find out just when the other party will be available for a return call from you. This process will get easier and more efficient as you and your secretary work together over the years.

Obviously, the person who should get through to you at one time of the day may need to be put off at others. Let's say you routinely set aside from 9:00 to 11:30 A.M. for writing and research. Your secretary should be instructed to disturb you only for emergencies (real, not fictional), family calls, or a call from the boss. All others will be told politely that you are "in conference," or unavailable to take the call at that time. Your secretary should ask when it would be convenient for you to return those calls he/she knows you want to return. By setting up a return call time, you have made it clear that the caller is important to you and that you will get back to him/her at a mutually agreeable time.

Running Interference for Yourself

What if you have no secretary? It's much more difficult to screen your own calls, but it can be done, if you do it right.

The first rule is to be cordial. If you care about the person but don't want to take the call at this time, you must make the caller feel that you really do want to speak with him/her but are just so jammed up with a very important project that you can't do it now. Setting up a time for a return call or in-person meeting is always a good idea because it respects the self-esteem of the caller and tells him/her that you value his/her time and conversation.

Uninvited Guests

The technique for dealing with uninvited guests is a bit more complicated because it is more difficult to get rid of someone who appears at your threshold, rather than on the phone.

Your secretary should screen all visitors for you. In order for this to work, your secretary's desk must be placed in a strategically appropriate position and you must not be within view. Otherwise, the visitor may simply march right into your office and make him/herself at home.

The Closed Door Defense

A closed door is your first line of defense and best protection against uninvited guests. It is a barrier that must be crossed. It must be knocked on before one can enter. It tells the world that you want privacy.

If someone barges in unannounced whom you don't want to see at that moment, the caller will probably ask if you have a minute, or if he/she is disturbing you. Don't hesitate to say "Yes" to the latter question. Or you may indicate that you are very busy and can only spare a moment. Once again we suggest setting up another time for meeting in order to respect the self-esteem of the person who interrupted you.

Try to Shorten Interruptions

If you have been interrupted, take charge of the exchange and set a time limit. If you have problems ending the visit, try saying something like, "Before I get back to what I was doing, is there anything else I can help you with?" or "This item is very important. Perhaps we should schedule another meeting at a time when I can concentrate on it better."

Don't Waste Others' Time

Finally, we'd like you to think not only of those who waste your time, but of those whose time you waste. Try not to drop in unannounced, be aware of the other person's time pressures, and be gracious about not outstaying your welcome.

19 · CRISES, CATASTROPHES, AND OTHER THINGS THAT CAN RUIN YOUR DAY

Dealing with crises and emergencies is always a problem, especially if you are busy with other matters and even more so if the crisis occurs during time which you had carefully scheduled for completion of other projects. But a Management P*R*O can balance conflicting priorities and organize each day for maximum, well-directed efficiency. In order to do that, the P*R*O system has to allow for crises. And it does.

Balance the Importance

The first thing a P*R*O will do is analyze the emergency. Is it a real crisis, or a lesser problem in coping that someone else wants you to take off his/her hands? You have to balance the value of what you are doing against the nature of the emergency.

Once again we remind you of the importance of being honest with your friends, family, and business associates regarding your priorities and your definition of an emergency. You can't expect others to respect your priorities unless you respect those priorities yourself and make them clear to others.

Of course, there are events which always qualify as emergencies—sudden grave illnesses, accidents, fire, threats of violence, etc. But think back on how many "emergencies" you have been dragged into solving that really weren't emergencies at all.

Coping With True Crises

In a true emergency, all other work must stop and you must deal only with the crisis or emergency, which becomes Number One on your P•R•O Scale.

Reprioritize, Reorganize, and Rethink

You must immediately reorganize and reprioritize in order to handle the emergency effectively and quickly.

Coping with Questionable Crises

Your secretary will often be able to decide whether a problem is an emergency requiring your immediate attention, or whether it can wait. But one technique that is surprisingly effective is to ask your caller directly if this really is a crisis that deserves interrupting your busy schedule. You'll be surprised how many times the answer will be no. Honesty and directness are often the best time-savers of all.

Don't Create Crises

We can unknowingly create crises ourselves by failing to anticipate or plan for contingencies. If you expect the unexpected and remember Murphy's Third Law—anything that *can* go wrong *will* go wrong—you will develop a plan for crisis management.

There are some people who seem to operate on a crisis level at all times. Studies have shown that the person who continually operates at a crisis pitch may be creating the catastrophe by letting tasks accumulate until they become critical, in order to feed the person's ego and increase his/her feeling of importance.

Don't Overreact

Everything is not necessarily a crisis and not all crises are created equal. Take time to think. Many so-called crises do not merit your personal attention and can be delegated and handled by someone else.

Allow Leeway

Try not to overplan each day. One top executive we know leaves 20 percent of the time unplanned each day in order to have room for unplanned events.

Maintain Priorities

In spite of a so-called crisis, you must resist the temptation to let apparently urgent minor items take precedence over major ones. This concentration on first priorities first is the essence of P*R*O Management.

Plan Ahead

After a crisis is past, you should take some time to think about planning ahead so that the same or a similar crisis will not occur again.

20 · MEETINGS

Meetings can absorb appalling quantities of time. However, a Management P•R•O understands meeting techniques and knows how to run an efficient, productive, time-effective meeting.

Before you call a meeting, always consider if the meeting is really necessary. Think about priorities. Will the meeting really be productive enough to justify stopping other work? Many meetings are unnecessary, and only result from failure to organize and delegate responsibilities effectively. But some meetings, of course, are necessary and unavoidable. The trick, very simply, is to avoid distractions and to keep the meeting as short as the situation permits.

Agenda

The first rule for an effective meeting is to have a printed agenda distributed prior to the meeting. The meeting leader should make it known that all agenda items have to be submitted, preferably in writing, by a given date. Attendees may or may not be permitted to request additional agenda items once the agenda is distributed, depending on the situation.

Set Time Parameters

Put a time limit on each item and try to limit discussion to the allotted time. An overall time limit on the meeting should also be established and strictly adhered to. Don't schedule a meeting to last more than an hour unless there's a very good reason.

Start Promptly

Make a habit of starting promptly. A late-starting meeting wastes everyone's time, and delaying the meeting for latecomers only rewards their tardiness. The Chair should begin the meeting promptly even if everyone has not arrived. If the Chair then demands an explanation of every latecomer, it should inspire promptness in the future.

Delegate Responsibility

Your agenda should name the person responsible for leading the discussion on each particular subject. The Chair may summarize the discussion.

After the matter has been concluded and an action decided upon, an individual should be named to take follow-up responsibility.

Circulation of Agenda and Minutes

It is often the case that someone doesn't need to attend a meeting, or actually can't attend, but needs to be aware of what transpired. In this case, the person should be on the circulation list for the agenda (which will also help him/her decide whether or not to attend the meeting) and, if there are meeting minutes, the person should receive a copy, whether or not he/she attended.

No Nonsense Meeting Tips

We'd like to suggest the following as excellent tips for successful and productive meetings:

1. All meetings must have an agenda, sent out in advance and strictly adhered to.
2. All meetings should have a clearly stated purpose, preferably written.
3. Only those people directly affected by the topic of the meeting should take the time to attend. Others can be kept informed by a meeting report or minutes.
4. Avoid regular meetings on a fixed schedule. Schedule meetings only when there is good reason for them.
5. Start on time, whether or not all attendees have arrived.

6. At the meeting, clearly state and assign follow-up duties with a timetable for completion.
7. Consider staggered attendance. Encourage attendees to stay only for items that directly affect them.
8. Schedule meetings at a time when they will interfere least with the day's productivity.
9. Complete and distribute the minutes of the meeting as quickly as possible.
10. Mark your calendar regarding due dates for follow-up reports.
11. Take inventory of all standing committees with a view to eliminating all but the most essential.

21 · ELEVEN COMMON TIME WASTERS AND THEIR CURES

A Management P•R•O leads by example. In this chapter, we'll show you how to overcome the eleven most common management time wasters.

1. Finish First Things First

Do first things first. Complete high P•R•O Scale items before you start another project. Do not leave high priority items incomplete. And remember to reward yourself when an item is finished, not before.

2. Distinguish Between the Urgent and the Important

Always do important items first. Crisis management is counterproductive and not all emergencies are real. Take time to analyze the urgent to see if it should take precedence over the important. Focus on your P•R•O Scale of priorities.

3. Attempting to Do Too Much

You can't do everything. Don't be unrealistic about your deadlines, and don't expect unrealistic miracles from others. Plan some leeway in your schedule. Try to keep Murphy's First and Second Laws in mind—(1) Nothing is as simple as it seems; and (2) Everything takes longer than you think. Combine these with that infamous Third Law—(3) If anything can go wrong, it will—and you have an excellent basis on which to allocate your time.

4. Failure to Make Decisions and Set Deadlines

A wrong decision is often better than no decision at all. At least, if you make a wrong decision, and action is begun on a project as a result, you will see your mistakes earlier and have time to correct them. No decision means no progress.

Similarly, you should impose deadlines to prevent procrastination. By fixing a time when something must be done, you can budget your time to ensure completion.

5. Failure to Say "No"

We all want to be agreeable to others and to appear endlessly energetic. Our first response to any request or demand is usually to say "Yes," even if we are so busy that it makes no sense at all to add another item to our roster.

Learning to say "No" graciously but firmly is an important part of being a Management P•R•O. If something is requested of you, take adequate time to consider whether you have the time (and desire) to assume the additional responsibility. If your answer is "No," always remember to give the requester the reason for your refusal.

6. Failure to Set Standards and Establish Controls

A lack of reporting standards and controls can lead to chaos. Make sure that you set standards of excellence by your example, and that those who work for and live with you understand how your system works.

7. Socializing

Socializing is fun and an essential part of life. However, socializing when you should be working is a time waster. Limit your socializing to appropriate times such as lunch or after work.

8. Using "In-Between" Time

We all have "in-between" spaces of time—two to ten minutes in between appointments or meetings. Use "in-between" time to make appointments, write short notes, prepare lists, read clippings, reorganize, or make a brief phone call.

9. Personal Disorganization—The Cluttered Desk Syndrome

A friend of ours has a sign on his immaculately clean desk that reads—"A clean desk is the sign of a cluttered mind." Of course, just the opposite is true. If your desk is cluttered with letters, research material, memos, lists, and other objects, it means that you have not done anything to expedite completion of those items and they are stagnating on your desk. Remember our three No Nonsense rules about paper—Toss It! File It! or Move It! And do it now!

10. No Need Always to be Perfect

Many tasks have to be done to perfection, but not all. Take note of which items in your day can be done in a less-than-perfect manner and still be acceptable. Concentrate your efforts and your perfection on those items that merit it.

11. Work Smarter, Not Harder

Take the time to think things through before you act in haste.

Focus on the goals and rewards you have set for yourself and with others; organize and list your priorities—and you will be a Management P•R•O.

INDEX

About the Authors

PHYLLIS C. KAUFMAN, the originator of the *No Nonsense Guides,* is a Philadelphia attorney and theatrical producer. A graduate of Brandeis University, she was an editor of the law review at Temple University School of Law. She is listed in *Who's Who in American Law, Who's Who of American Women, Who's Who in Finance and Industry,* and *Foremost Women of the Twentieth Century.*

ARNOLD CORRIGAN, noted financial expert, is the author of *How Your IRA Can Make You a Millionaire* and is a frequent guest on financial talk shows. A senior officer of a large New York investment advisory firm, he holds Bachelor's and Master's degrees in economics from Harvard and has written for *Barron's* and other financial publications.

